JEDEDIAH SMITH

EXPLORER IN THE AMERICAN WEST

by Dennis Fertig

Boston, Massachusetts
Chandler, Arizona
Glenview, Illinois
Upper Saddle River, New Jersey

Illustrations
Opener, 1, 2, 3, 4, 9, 12, 14, 15 John White; 13 Joe LeMonnier.

Photographs
Every effort has been made to secure permission and provide appropriate credit for photographic material.
The publisher deeply regrets any omission and pledges to correct errors called to its attention in subsequent editions.

Unless otherwise acknowledged, all photographs are the property of Pearson Education, Inc.

Photo locators denoted as follows: Top (T), Center (C), Bottom (B), Left (L), Right (R), Background (Bkgd)

3 Dynamic Graphics, 2007/Thinkstock; 5 Prints & Photographs Division, LC-USZ61-1473/Library of Congress; 6 Curtis (Edward S.) Collection, Prints & Photographs Division, LC-USZ62-130160/Library of Congress; 7 Stockbyte/Thinkstock; 8 Hemera Technologies/Thinkstock; 10 Comstock/Thinkstock; 11 Prints & Photographs Division, LC-USZ62-113676/Library of Congress.

ISBN-13: 978-0-328-67651-4
ISBN-10:   0-328-67651-9

3 4 5 6 7 8 9 10 V0FL 15 14 13 12

Grizzly Attack!

In 1823, Jedediah Smith led a group of **trappers** through the woods. Suddenly, an angry grizzly bear attacked. In seconds, Smith was horribly injured. The men with Smith quickly shot and killed the bear. But would Smith survive? They were hundreds of miles away from help. But Smith thought quickly and ordered one man to find a needle and thread. The man quickly stitched up Smith's wounds. Somehow Smith survived. Within days, he was leading his men again. He was leading them even farther from safety.

Why did Smith risk his life to **explore** new lands? This is the story of Jedidiah Smith, who became one of the country's most important explorers of the West.

Many people were inspired by explorers Lewis and Clark.

Inspired by Lewis and Clark

Jedediah Smith was born in New York in 1799. During his youth, his family moved farther west to Pennsylvania and then Ohio. Smith grew up hunting, fishing, and trapping in the nearby woods and streams.

Smith could read and write. This was not the case with many people in the early 1800s. Smith especially enjoyed reading the journals of the explorers Meriwether Lewis and William Clark.

From 1804 to 1806, Lewis and Clark had explored a huge area that was then new to the United States. Their journals inspired many people, including Smith.

A Young Trapper

When Smith was 22, he dreamed of going west into lands that only Native American people knew. He also hoped to earn a good living by trapping beavers and selling their fur skins.

Beaver furs were so valuable they were known as "brown gold." Trappers of these furs could become rich—or die trying. The work was extremely dangerous.

Smith arrived in St. Louis around the time an ad appeared in a local newspaper. It was addressed to "**Enterprising** Young Men." Businessman and trapper William Ashley was looking for 100 brave men to work for his beaver-trapping business.

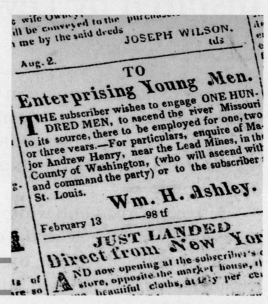

William Ashley's ad

Trappers moved up and down rivers on boats designed to move easily through shallow waters.

Smith understood the dangers of this work. Yet Smith answered the ad, proving to Ashley that he was an enterprising man. Smith's adventures were about to begin.

In the spring of 1822, Smith was part of a group of trappers that headed up the Missouri River to trap beavers. Trappers were also known as mountain men. They were a rough bunch who risked their lives for brown gold. They were known for spending every penny they had earned. From the beginning, however, Smith was different. He didn't share their bad habits. Unlike most other trappers, he could read and write. Eventually, he even taught himself mapmaking. He also knew how to hold on to his money.

A Bloody Battle

Nearly 20 years earlier, Smith's heroes, Lewis and Clark, had gone up the Missouri River. They had hoped it was part of a water route to the Pacific Ocean. While the Missouri River did head northwest, it didn't actually reach the ocean. In fact, Lewis and Clark never found the water route they were looking for.

During Smith's time, however, the Missouri was the route that trappers took most often. The river flowed through huge unmapped territories. Many Native American people lived along the river. And many of them did not trust trappers, who did not always deal with them fairly.

One day in 1823, Smith and the trappers were trading with Native American people called the Arikara. Something went wrong and a fight broke out. Many trappers were killed. As survivors raced to safety, Smith fought to protect them.

This photograph from the early 1900s shows an Arikara man named White Shield.

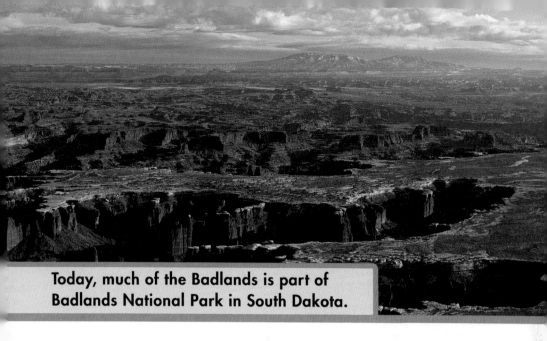

Today, much of the Badlands is part of Badlands National Park in South Dakota.

Becoming a Leader

Ashley knew that using the Missouri River might be dangerous, but he didn't expect a battle. Now, he decided to travel by horseback on land.

Ashley split his men into two groups. He would lead one group. For the second, he chose Jedediah Smith. Smith was young and not as experienced as others. But Ashley had seen Smith's bravery and leadership firsthand. He trusted this young man.

Smith led his group though the Badlands, an area of what is now South Dakota. In the 1820s, much of it was land that only Native American people had ever seen. It was hot and **arid**. Little grew there. As they traveled, the men suffered. Without water, both the horses and the men struggled to survive.

Weeks later, the grizzly bear attack took place. Smith's quick thinking and calmness after the bear attack made him famous among mountain men.

That winter, Smith's group stayed with a Native American group called the Crow. Trappers had long looked for a way to cross the Rocky Mountains. The Crow told Smith about a pass that could be taken across the mountains.

The rugged Rockies

Smith Opens the Way West

In the spring of 1824, Smith located the pass that became known as South Pass. It was a fairly easy way to cross the rugged Rockies. Years later the pass became an important part of the Oregon Trail. Eventually, more than a quarter of a million **pioneers** used South Pass to reach the West.

Smith's bravery and hard work brought him business success. In 1826, he attended a **rendezvous**, a gathering of trappers. He and two partners bought Ashley's business. Then, Smith's partners left to hunt in more familiar territory. Smith, however, decided to explore. For four years, he travelled throughout the West. His discoveries helped show Americans which routes to use and which to avoid in reaching the wonders of the West.

To California

Smith's group began the **expedition** by traveling past the Great Salt Lake, in what is today Utah. Their route took them down the length of Utah and then across Nevada toward California.

Smith hoped to find a river that people believed flowed from the Great Salt Lake to the Pacific Ocean. The river appeared on many old maps. If Smith could find the river, it might be easy for him and his men to make their way to California. But Smith couldn't find the river. In fact, his explorations over the next years helped prove that such a river didn't even exist.

Smith's group traveled along the edge of the Great Basin, a desert area in today's Utah and Nevada.

A beautiful valley in California

Smith's expedition crossed the edges of a large **desert** known only to Native Americans. This land, the Great Basin, had few plants and little water. Smith called it "the country of starvation." As the group traveled, they were helped by Mojave Native Americans, who acted as guides.

After they left the desert, the weary trappers crossed the San Bernardino Mountains. On the other side, they discovered a beautiful valley near what is now Los Angeles. The men had entered what would become the state of California. They were the first American group to reach California by land.

California was then part of Mexico. The Mexican government feared that Smith was an American spy and ordered him to leave. Smith left Los Angeles, but not California. Smith took his men and headed north. They spent the winter trapping beavers.

California Once Again

The trappers had had a successful winter. They'd trapped so much beaver that their horses couldn't carry the load of furs through the spring snows. Smith decided to set up a camp for most of the group. Then he took two men and began an amazing journey to the rendezvous.

The three crossed the Sierra Nevada. They were probably the first people to travel over these steep mountains. Then they crossed the Great Basin. They were the first non–Native Americans to do so. However, the heat, and lack of food and water, made the journey exhausting. They made it, barely, to the rendezvous.

Smith stayed just ten days before he left with a fresh group of trappers. They needed to get back to the men that had been left behind. Smith followed nearly the same route that he'd taken before.

Exploration by Jedediah Smith

CANADA

Fort Vancouver

Columbia R.

Snake R. South Pass

rendezvous

ROCKY MOUNTAINS

Badlands

Missouri R.

Mississippi R.

Great Salt Lake

Great Basin

SIERRA NEVADA

San Francisco

Colorado R.

Great Plains

St. Louis

Arkansas R.

Los Angeles

PACIFIC
OCEAN

MEXICO

- ▬▬ Early Exploration, 1822–1823
- ▬▬ First Trip to California, 1826–1827
- ▬▬ Second Trip to California, 1827–1828
- ▬▬ Northern California to Washington, 1828
- *Present day boundaries are shown.*

On this trip, no Native Americans aided Smith. Instead, the Mojave people were angry because other trappers had treated them poorly. In an attack on the Colorado River, Mojave warriors killed more than half the members of Smith's new expedition.

After that, the remaining trappers once again struggled across harsh country. When they reached California, Mexico once again ordered Smith to leave. Once again, instead of leaving, he headed farther north to his camp in northern California. Smith continued to **blaze** new trails.

The End of Many Trails

Smith covered more than 800 miles and reached Fort Vancouver in what is now the state of Washington. This trip by land from California to Washington was another first for Americans. Along the way, Smith noted that the land was rich and filled with animals for hunting. He later reported this to the U.S. government.

However, this trip turned tragic. A Native American group attacked, and 15 trappers were killed. Only Smith and three others reached safety.

On his expeditions, Smith had survived three major battles with Native American people, a bear attack, and the deaths of many friends. He had finally had enough.

Hundreds of thousands of pioneers would later travel on the Oregon Trail, following a route partly mapped out by Smith.

At the rendezvous in 1830, Smith sold his business. Now a wealthy man, he returned to St. Louis. However, in the spring of 1831, he took one last trip along the Santa Fe Trail. He wanted to help some traders move goods west. While alone scouting for water, Smith ran into a group of Comanche Native Americans. For some reason, a brief gunfight occurred. Smith was suddenly and unexpectedly in a fourth battle with Native Americans. In just seconds, two men died. One was the Comanche chief. The other one was Smith.

Smith was only 32 years old. He had led an explorer's life like his heroes, Lewis and Clark. He had bravely gone to places few others had. He had mapped these places, written about them, and urged others to visit them. He was an enterprising explorer who helped open the West for others to settle.

Glossary

arid dry

blaze to open up a new trail or path

desert an area that gets little rain or snow

enterprising showing energy, leadership, and courage

expedition a journey by a group of explorers

explore to travel to or investigate new places

pioneer one of the first settlers in a place

rendezvous a gathering of mountain men, or fur trappers

trapper someone who traps, or catches, animals and sells their fur